about editing

an essential guide for authors

Sallianne Hines

A GRASSLANDS PRESS publication

www.salliannehines.com

Cover design by Rachael Ritchey

Interior design/formatting by Sallianne Hines

www.quinnediting.com

ISBN 97989862078-1-0 (paperback)

ISBN 97989862078-3-4 (hardcover)

ISBN 97989862078-0-3 (ebook)

contents

why this book, and why me?

Why this book?

Editing is an important milestone on any path to publishing. A savvy author understands how editing can benefit their own project. With so many publishing paths available nowadays, it is more important than ever that you, the author, have a good understanding of publishing procedures. Your book's success depends on it.

There are many good, comprehensive books written for editors, but not many books that explain, in common working terms, the ins and outs of editing at the level most authors need.

The purpose of this book is to provide a working overview of editing, and to dispel some of the misconceptions. You will learn about the types of editing, when each might be needed, how to choose an editor, and how to save on editing expenses.

Proper editing raises the quality and credibility of your manuscript. It can do the same for your submission packages, marketing materials, social media posts, and websites. Many authors overlook these crucial advantages. Even if you are aiming for traditional publication, your project will benefit greatly from professional and timely editing.

Why me?

Some people spot errors in almost anything they read. I am one of those people. Errors just pop out at me. So some of my skill is an inborn talent. But editing involves much more than detecting typos.

I established Quinn Editing in 2015 but my editing experience goes back to the early 1970s. When working for small and mid-sized publications, one wears many hats. Not only did I design page layouts and write feature stories, I also did lots of reorganizing, rewriting, and proofreading of articles and submissions.

Next came a deep dive into the nuances and finer skills of editing via a combination of self-education, experience, and professional training. I continue my on-going learning with professional associations and webinars. While many countries have some kind of certification process to document an editor's expertise, the US has no such system. Here, anyone can hang out their shingle and claim to be an editor. Authors need to be cautious and informed when they hire an editor.

I have edited many well-written manuscripts and others that needed a lot of work. I've also helped some less-informed but talented authors, such as one who handed me a pile of printed-out social media posts and said, "Here, is this anything?"—out of which we made a book of witticisms. Another author presented me with an incredible four-volume project—typed on a manual typewriter. I transcribed and edited that one, a brilliant historical saga. I know how to organize and polish a project to brilliance, whether it's in rough shape or well-done enough to just need a few touch-ups.

As an indie author myself, I know firsthand the concerns authors have—quality, budget, preserving their voice, when to fit editing into the writing/publishing process—and this volume offers recommendations about those things as well as some tried and true strategies to help you get the best editing at an affordable price.

My hope is that you are successful, and that this book proves a useful tool in learning how quality editing can smooth the way for that success—however you define it—with your present book and any yet to come.

The hook for me, as an editor, is the joy in helping a raw piece of work grow into a great beauty that speaks in a unique and powerful voice—your best voice. I'm honored to be a partner in any author's publishing process.

Sallianne Hines
www.quinnediting.com

chapter
one

Writing & Publishing from an Editing Perspective

THE GOAL with all editing is to preserve and enhance the writer's unique voice while clarifying the message for the reader's understanding and enjoyment.

Any creative project meant to be shared with the world—whether a novel, an article or essay, a short story, or an author website—needs a fresh pair of eyes on it first. It's the best way to ensure the clearest author voice and the highest quality of craft—both vital for effective communication of a story or an idea.

Editing might be described as cleaning and polishing your original piece of work to make it ready for publication. At its most basic, it is the process in which you take your first draft and strive to make it flawless. It is much more than correcting spelling, capitalization, and punctuation—as you will learn later in *Types of Editing*.

Authors also need to know how self-editing works in tandem with professional editing. Both are important to the success of any book.

A reminder as we begin: be sure you have and use a system of *multiple* backups all the way through your process.

- Back up on an auxiliary drive on a regular basis.
- In addition to that, email that updated version to yourself. Authors should have different personal and professional email addresses, so send it from one to the other.
- You can also email a copy to a trusted friend to simply hold for you in case you ever need it.
- Create a digital backup on a Cloud server.
- Make sure each backup version is *clearly labeled* in whatever system makes sense to you (V1, V2, or Version A, Version B, or Book Name June 2023, Book Name August 2023, etc.) Hopefully you will never need your backups, but if you ever do you will be unbelievably grateful to have them.

Before we go further, you should understand there are THREE STAGES OF PUBLISHING, and there are editing needs unique to each stage.

- STAGE ONE is writing the first draft and getting all your ideas down in some kind of order.
- STAGE TWO is all about revising, self-editing, getting outside feedback, then hiring a professional

editor to elevate your creation into publishable form. *This second stage often takes the longest.*

- STAGE THREE includes choosing your publishing path, formatting, cover creation, uploading to sales sites, creating author pages on those sales sites, and then marketing your project. *This stage is ongoing for as long as your book is for sale and you will be tweaking and updating all these things over time.*

As an author you should also have a good understanding of the various PATHS TO PUBLISHING. Traditional publishing and vanity publishing are the classic modes. Self-publishing has grown tremendously, in numbers and in quality, and is now fully acceptable and viable. The new players are hybrid publishing and service providers.

The path you choose affects the editing your project will need.

If you are set on trying the traditional publishing path, once you secure a *legitimate* agent and/or publisher, much of your editing will be handled by them. Most of your editing needs will occur before that, in your submission materials, to help you clear the huge hurdle of being chosen and signed. Just be sure you are accepted by a *legitimate* agent and a *legitimate* publisher, not a service provider or vanity press in disguise. There are lots of scams out there. If it seems too good to be true, it probably is.

We will expand on publishing paths later in this book.

chapter
two

Why a Professional Editor?

EVERY WRITER NEEDS AN EDITOR. Some claim they don't—but if you look closely at their books it is usually obvious that they don't realize how much they don't know. In addition to knowledge of grammar, a professional editor has special training in literary form, syntax, genre styles and expectations, and is skilled at polishing the voice of the writer without changing it.

Your editor is your partner in publishing at several steps along the way. Besides honing your current project, feedback from a good editor can help you improve your writing skills and increase your likelihood of ongoing success.

NO ONE CAN OR SHOULD BE THE ONLY EDITOR OF THEIR OWN WORK

I am an editor *and* a writer. We writers know what we meant to write, so even if our actual written words don't accurately communicate the idea, our brain will still understand it and complete it. We won't see our own errors or omissions.

ISN'T EDITING EXPENSIVE?

Yes, it can be.

But think of your editing expense as an investment in the development of your product—your book, your website, your marketing materials, even your career as an author.

All investments involve costs, whether you are creating a book, building a house, or manufacturing a product. One way or another, you will need to invest some money—and a great deal of time—to get your book published and out into the world. You've already put months or years into your project so don't short-change it at the end. Poor-quality editing or no editing will cost you big bucks in the long run with lost sales and a tarnished brand identity.

But be assured, there *are* ways to maximize your investment and keep costs minimal while still reaping the benefits of quality editing.

Good editing will not change your book or your writer voice. I like to compare editing to a song playing on the radio. If the radio isn't tuned in all the way there is static, which interferes with the enjoyment of even the best song, story, or interview. Editing removes the static so you can communicate with clarity—still in your own unique voice.

An editor can help you achieve a higher level of quality in your writing, whether you are self-publishing or seeking an agent/publisher. Good editing reveals your writing at its best.

If you are an indie (an independent publisher or a self-publisher), the quality of your final product will boost your initial win of readers, garner the loyalty of those readers, and provide positive word-of-mouth advertising for your book—and that's the best kind!

Should you hope to publish traditionally, submitting well-written and clean work can only increase your chances of being taken on by an agent or publisher—a huge hurdle on the traditional publishing path.

CAN'T BETA READERS EDIT?

No. The role of a beta reader in the publishing process is completely different from that of an editor.

A beta reader should be a member of your target audience who reads widely but especially reads in your genre. They should represent the readers who will buy your book.

The beta's job is to read your work as a consumer would, in order to point out to you—before you publish—any problems that interfere with their reading enjoyment. More on beta readers later in *Self-Editing Comes First*.

While there are several tools and strategies that can assist you in book development, there really is no substitute for a professional editor.

chapter
three

Proper Document Setup Saves Time
& Money

FOLLOWING standard document setup will save you money
on editing, and allow you to interact in a professional manner
with other service providers, agents, and publishers.

Editing is intense, and having a standard format to work from
is easier all around. If your document is ready for the editor in this
way, they won't have to spend time getting it into standard format
for editing. As with most things, time is money.

Familiarize yourself with *Track Changes* in Microsoft Word
because that is what a professional editor will use. All edits and
comments will be indicated on your manuscript and in the
margins. For the edits you can select *Accept* or *Reject*. So easy! You
will probably need to handle the comments separately.

It helps to set up your document correctly when you begin
writing, but you can make that happen later too. Every version of
Word is different so I can't give you exact settings. If you need
further help, ask in online writing groups or check YouTube for

helpful videos about Word. Here are some guidelines for setting up your document.

- Use *Style Sheets* in Word. That way, any of your parameters can be easily changed. For example, if you want to write your book in some other font and in a large size, just change the *Text Style* in your Word *Style Sheet*. Then, before you submit to an editor or formatter, you can easily change it back to the standard size and font (*see below*). Plus, using *Style Sheets* will save problems, delays, and extra expense when you get to formatting.
- Create your document in 12-point black Times New Roman (or similar common serif font such as Century or Garamond). Fonts come in serif style (with the little hooks at the ends of letters), sans serif style (straight edges at ends of letters), and a variety of scripts (like cursive writing or calligraphy). Use a common serif font (serif fonts are usually easier to read) that everyone would have in their font list to reduce the chance of glitches. This makes it easier for your alpha and beta readers as well as your editors and formatters.
- Make your document flush left and double spaced. No color, unless you are paying for color on your interior pages in the final printing. Document size should be 8.5" x 11" (or A4) with 1" margins all around, *no matter what size you want your final book pages to be or what fonts you want on the final printed pages*. Interior

book styling is done later, in formatting. It is not done now.

- Use a single space after periods, not two spaces. Extra spaces will all have to be removed, at your expense. The double spacing after periods went out of favor more than twenty years ago. It's much easier to do it correctly from the start.

- Indent paragraphs—or not—according to your genre, but *do not use tabs or spaces to indent.* Set up the indent in the *Paragraph* part of *Style Sheets* in Word. Tabs or spaces will have to be removed, at your expense. They will mess up the formatting. Generally, fiction uses a .5 indent and no space between paragraphs. Nonfiction can be indented or not, but if you don't indent then you need extra space between paragraphs. Again, set this up in *Style Sheets* by designating how many points before or after a return—*do not use extra or double returns.* Memoirs and other creative nonfiction can also go either way as far as indents. Look at traditionally printed books in your genre—that are recent—and copy what they did. You want your book to fit in with other professionally produced books.

- If your book is nonfiction, section it into easily-read segments. Subheads and indented sections, along with bullets, can be helpful. Set these up in *Style Sheets.*

- Chapter heads and subheads can be in bold or italic or capital letters. Set these up individually in *Style Sheets.* Do not use underlining, especially in fiction. And use italic sparingly—long blocks of italic type are hard to read.

- If you want a letter or an email in your book to appear in a different font or in italic, set this up in your *Style Sheets*. You choose the names of these items in *Style Sheets*, so you could call it Letter Font or Email Font, or whatever makes sense to you.
- Use *Insert Page Break* in Word at the end of a chapter. *Do not use multiple returns*; these will have to be removed, at your expense.
- Send your editor the manuscript as a single Word document, not as chapters, unless this has been previously arranged. This will save organizing time for the editor and save money for you.

Following these guidelines may also reduce your cost for formatting, which comes after all editing is complete (except for proofreading, which is done after formatting).

chapter
four

Self-Editing Comes First

SEVERAL PEOPLE MAY BE INVOLVED in your editing process besides a professional editor or two. It makes sense to employ all the tools available to make your book the best it can be *before* you hire a professional editor. Extensive self-editing can definitely reduce your overall editing expense, if you know how to do it effectively.

SELF-EDITING THE FIRST DRAFT

Be aware that the editing/revising process requires a completely different mindset than the creative stage of writing the first draft, especially when writing fiction. It is usually recommended to avoid editing while you are writing the first draft for this very reason—it can interrupt your creative flow. If issues nag at you while you write, just type a note to yourself right in your manuscript, which you can address later. Then write on.

· · ·

SELF-EDITING THE EARLY DRAFTS,
    BEFORE "OUTSIDE" INPUT

Much early editing will be done by you, the author, in the form of revisions. These early revisions will be based on your own repeated re-reading of your draft. You might make one pass through your book to check the timeline of events to be sure there are no holes or conflicts. In another pass you might examine dialogue to be sure it is realistic and that each character speaks in a unique way. You might wish to evaluate your narrative descriptions—do you have too much or not enough? Another pass could be reviewing the development or arc of your main character.

At this point, some authors like to print out a version or two and use a highlighter to indicate the various things they are reviewing. For example, maybe all description sections are highlighted in green, all dialogue might be indicated by pink, or the dialogue of different characters might be indicated by different colors. This also helps you look for a good balance of narrative versus dialogue. For more about color-coding techniques, see *Non-Tech Self-Editing*, in the section just ahead.

If your book is nonfiction, in your early drafts you are looking for a sensible hierarchy of points supporting your main premise with strong organization and clear language so the reader comes away with a good understanding of your message.

Be sure to see the *Non-Tech Self-Editing Help* and *Let Basic Technology Work for You* sections just ahead for more self-editing ideas. Some techniques can be used both before and after "outside" input, and can help organize your mindset as you revise.

When working on early drafts it makes no sense to edit for mechanical things like spelling or punctuation. Doing so takes your focus away from your story. You want to concentrate on the power of your story or nonfiction idea at this point. Don't waste time correcting typos on writing that may later be revised or removed.

During the writing of your first draft, or while you are working on early drafts, you may choose to enlist a developmental/content editor (see *Types of Editing*). If you want this kind of editing help, get it during these early drafts.

SELF-EDITING EARLY DRAFTS,
   AFTER "OUTSIDE" INPUT

Authors employ various timetables as to when they want input from outsiders such as alpha and beta readers, critique partners, and critique groups. With these kinds of early input, it is helpful to recognize that if two or three of them flag the same problem, it is probably worth your concentrated attention to rewrite or remove. Otherwise, you will need to decide if these reader comments support your vision for your book.

An ALPHA READER is the first "outside" person to read the entire book straight through and give an opinion (unless you are using a developmental editor). An alpha reader is not necessarily a writer. This reader should be one who enjoys reading your genre and reads widely so they have a broad idea of what makes an interesting book.

- The alpha reader is looking at the overall plot and timeline for holes and conflicts, at the character development, and at the overall interest your story generates. If your antagonist is weak or your protagonist has no realistic motivation for their actions, you need to go back to the drawing board for major revisions.
- If your book is nonfiction, the alpha reader evaluates your premise and message, then determines if the way you have organized the book brings your message across in the strongest way. Organization is often the biggest challenge with nonfiction.

When the alpha reader has completed their pass, you decide what, if any, of their input is useful, then you go back and revise your manuscript accordingly.

⊏⊐

While writing or during early revisions, some authors share their work with a CRITIQUE PARTNER or CRITIQUE GROUP. These are fellow writers, preferably writing in your genre or at least widely read. Authors often share smaller chunks of their book with these helpers—or the group may all read each other's work in progress and make comments on things like style, organization, and effectiveness/craft of the writing in such areas as character development, pacing, plot holes, timeline, lack of or excess narration or description, and unrealistic or unnatural dialogue.

- When sharing excerpts, it can be helpful to let the readers/listeners know what kind of feedback you want, such as questions about a character or deciding if your dialogue is realistic.
- Pick this person or group carefully. Do they have skills you respect? Do you find their feedback helpful? Can they be trusted to not pirate your ideas? I have found most other writers very helpful in my writing journey but do keep your antennae up.

As the author, you decide which of this critique seems valuable. Then you go back and revise.

Skilled, experienced, well-instructed BETA READERS can be invaluable. They are the second "outside" readers of your entire book in one pass—they read it as a reader would. Betas are usually power readers within your genre. They are not editors. They are not trained in literary style. As members of your target audience, their suggestions help you revise in ways that best satisfy that very audience.

- They may or may not be fellow writers, but not all of them should be writers.
- You'll want to schedule three or more beta readers. Unfortunately, not all those who agree to read will actually complete the task so ask a few more than you hope to get. If someone doesn't complete the read, ask

them where they stopped. Even that input can be
helpful.

- Betas may know something bothers them as they read,
but often don't know what it is or how to fix it; they
just point it out to you. It will be your job to figure
that out and repair it, or that of a developmental
editor who might be helping you.

- If two or more betas hone in on the same problem,
that is worth your focused attention and some
rewriting or adjustments.

- I advise providing your beta readers with a short list of
questions that cannot be answered with "Yes" or
"No." You can provide these *before* they read, but I
have also found the questions often helpful *after* the
read, so you know what "stuck with" your reader.

Questions betas address might include:

- In fiction: Who was your favorite character and why?
Are there plot holes? Are there inconsistencies that
confuse the reader? Is the timeline muddled? Which
part of the story did you find boring, that you wanted
to skip over? What was it about the beginning of the
story that you found compelling? Or did you have
trouble getting into the story? At what point did you
become fully engaged in the story? Were you satisfied
with the conclusion of the story—why or why not? If
you did not finish reading, where did you stop
and why?

- In nonfiction: Does the presentation confuse the reader? Does the message get across? What was the most memorable takeaway? Are the takeaways what you, the author, intended? Are readers pulled on board by your verbal and visual presentation?

Beta readers should not be looking for typos or poor sentence structure. They are not trained to do this. Their job is to give your book a trial run—before it goes live with indie publishing, or before you submit it to an agent or publisher in hopes of traditional publishing.

Many authors offer their alpha and beta readers a free copy of the book in return for their help.

NON-TECH SELF-EDITING TECHNIQUES

There are lots of ways to save money on editing costs by availing yourself of special self-editing techniques. Here are a few ideas.

- *Change your text font and size in Style Sheets.* This brings a fresh perspective to words you have seen *so* many times. Go ahead—read and revise in 18 point Noteworthy or 20-point Eras and see what you discover.
- *Color-coding strategies* involve printing out your manuscript and then using color to mark different types of items to review. Maybe you highlight all dialog in blue and go through your book evaluating

only the dialog. Does the story hold together? You might highlight all the description passages in pink and, when reading through the whole book, decide if you have too little or too much pink. Is a lot of that description repetitive? You might highlight one character in purple and read through only the purple to assess that character's development and arc. Does it make sense? Does it backtrack in confusing ways? Is the character arc weak or nonexistent? This technique helps the author focus on one aspect of writing and not be distracted by other issues. You can address those other issues on the next self-editing pass.

- *The support of family and friends is great*, but many authors don't find the input of family and friends helpful. Of course, there are exceptions. Perhaps a friend or family member could read your book aloud to you while you take notes. Or you could suggest they wait until the book is published and then read it and write a review.

With any and all input, in the end you must use your own judgement, as the author, to determine what ideas best suit your particular story and your vision for it.

LET BASIC TECHNOLOGY WORK FOR YOU

I'm not talking about the intricacies of coding, but simple things available in Word that will save you time or make better use of your time, help you improve the quality of your book, and help you reduce your editing costs.

FIND & REPLACE—This feature can save you loads of time. Here are some ways you can make it work for you.

- *Change character or place names.* If one of your characters is named Jenny, and you later decide to change her name to Laura, just enter these in the *Find and Replace* boxes. You can do a "blanket" change to replace all instances, or you can have Word take you to each instance in the manuscript to be sure you want to change it. Be aware, Word can't really "think." It might pick up on part of a word and change instances of that. For example, if you wanted to change Ben to John, it might change the word "beneficial" too. Be aware of this if you choose the *Change All* option.
- *Search for crutch words or phrases.* These are the words or phrases you overuse. I tend to use "just" a lot, so I search for all instances of "just" and decide, one by one, whether each usage is appropriate or not. Many authors search for the word "that," because it is one of the most overused words in manuscripts. It tends to make our writing wordy and cumbersome. In one book I read, to show the character's angst or frustration, the author used the phrase "he ran his hands through his hair" so many times I wondered if he would have any hair left at the end of the book! I

wish that author had searched for crutch/repetitive phrases.

- Evaluate usage of *filter phrases* like "he thought." These words are often not needed, or they may be repetitive. They tend to distance your reader from the action.
- Find and delete the *Accidental Double Period*. Enter two periods and a space, then replace that with one period and a space.
- Close up a *Double Space After a Period*. Enter a period and two spaces, then replace it with a period and one space.

HAVE YOUR COMPUTER READ TO YOU—The computer reads *only* what is there, and *everything* that is there. You will not believe how helpful it can be to hear your own words, as they are actually written, read back to you. Not only does it pick up errors or omissions, but hearing the rhythm and pace of your writing will likely inspire more of your own revisions.

- There are various ways to set up the computer read-aloud feature, depending on your version of Word and if you are on a PC or a Mac. You can use Word's *Help* menu or you can Google for tutorials.
- You can choose the speed at which the computer reads, and even the voice. I write British historical novels and specify a British woman's voice to read to me. You can pause as you go along, making edits and revisions or typing in notes to yourself to address later.

LOOK AT WHAT IS FLAGGED BY WORD—not that Word is always correct, because it isn't—but it does flag things like misspellings in red and grammatically questionable words in blue (or however your colors are set up). Read through your manuscript and take note of these. They are easy enough to fix yourself and doing so will save you money on editing. If Word continually flags unusual names that are spelled correctly, you can add these to Word's dictionary so it won't keep flagging them.

CONSIDER COMPUTER APPS AND PROGRAMS—New writing and editing programs are constantly being developed. Most have some level that is free, but that usually has limits and may or may not be worth your time.

- Ask fellow writers who use them and get recommendations. Some of the better-known programs are ProWritingAid, Grammarly, and Scrivener.
- Do be aware that these programs have limitations in their accuracy. You still need to evaluate each change suggested.
- While these programs can reduce some of your editing load and thus reduce the cost of editing, they certainly cannot replace a professional edit. By you catching and repairing the mundane typos and spellings, your human editor can concentrate on the deeper issues in your manuscript—so you'll get more for your money.

SEARCH FOR AND USE TECHNOLOGY TUTORIALS—
Don't discount the help available from online tutorials on places
like YouTube. These are often more helpful than the *Help* menu
in a software program. Use it for things like how to do page
numbers in Word, how to set up *Style Sheets*, or how to get your
computer to read aloud to you.

THESAURUS—Don't forget to use this handy feature. Not that
you want all manner of complicated words littering your project—
but when you need ideas for a verb more interesting than "walk,"
you will find all kinds of ideas in your thesaurus.

- Choose a *strong, specific verb* and then delete
  meaningless adverbs. An example might be changing
  "he walked slowly down the street" to "he ambled
  down the street" or "he shuffled down the street"—
  different impressions can be expressed based on the
  character's demeanor and style of movement. A
  specific word communicates so much more than a
  generic word.
- When you have *too many descriptive adjectives* for a
  noun, they tend to dilute each other, and your writing
  looks amateurish. Find sharper more specific words in
  your Thesaurus, then use just one or two good
  adjectives instead of three or four mediocre ones. An
  example might be changing "he wore a sleek,

fashionable, well-tailored new suit" to "he sported a natty suit." Stronger words give your writing much more punch and a more colorful visual impression.

You'll be surprised how using just a few technological helpers can upgrade your writing and speed up your self-editing and revision process. By fixing everything that you can yourself, you will cut down on the time your editor needs to spend on those same tasks. Do you really need to pay an editor to remove double periods or double spaces? Certainly not. Use your editing dollars to buy their more advanced professional expertise instead.

Evaluate your results and input, and use as you see fit—not all of it will be the right choice for your book or project. Too much feedback, especially if it is not professional, can be confusing and even overwhelming.

It is important to complete self-editing before you hire a professional editor. It helps you get your manuscript into the best shape possible so you can enjoy the full benefit of a professional edit. You may be surprised at how much editing you can handle yourself.

chapter
five

Types of Professional Editing &
When to Use Them

TO MAKE the best use of your editing budget, you need to understand the different types of editing and which will benefit your project at any given stage of development. There is an order in which the types of editing need to take place. It makes no sense —time-wise or cost-wise—to do detailed grammar corrections on passages that may yet be deleted or completely rewritten.

You can choose to bypass some of these editing stages, but you must be aware of what you are doing and why, and understand how it will impact the final quality of your book.

Once your manuscript is the best you can make it on your own, you are ready for professional editing. Exactly when you do this is determined by what kind of editing you need.

DEVELOPMENTAL OR CONTENT EDITING (also known as Structural or Substantive Editing)

That's a lot of words for this very comprehensive type of edit.

Timeline varies. Each developmental editor will specify what works best for them. The timeframe also depends on whether you hire a complete developmental edit or an editorial assessment or a manuscript critique (*described in more detail just ahead*). You need to decide which will be most beneficial for your book.

Developmental editing is the content phase, the "big picture" —it is an overall look at your project. It can even be done before you write (as you outline), or at specific points while you write, as noted above.

This is your earliest edit. It is likely undertaken after your first draft, or maybe after you have incorporated your first batch of beta reader suggestions. This edit deals with the structure of your book and how it works together as a whole.

As a broad, comprehensive assessment of your work, it looks at and provides specific advice for developing a compelling hook, more engaging characters, a plot without holes, a practical time-line of events, better overall pacing, and a strong narrative voice. The appropriateness of how your premise, theme, and style meet genre expectations is also evaluated. Here are some areas assessed in a developmental edit.

- For fiction, this edit examines your story and character arcs and how they all work together, your plot and setting, clarity of theme, and consistency in characterization, voice, and style—scene by scene.
- Choices of which tense (past or present) and which point of view (first, second, types of third person/omniscient) and single or multiple POVs are examined and established.

- Linear, dual, or other timelines are solidified.
- Other questions addressed might be: Does your protagonist have a defined character arc? A believable motivation? Does your plot hold together? Are the stakes meaningful? Is the beginning bogged down by too much description or backstory? Does your pace sag in the middle? Is the story climax powerful enough?
- For nonfiction, this level of editing helps you organize your information in the way most helpful to readers, to render your message clearly and powerfully. Is your message presented in a cohesive way? Are key questions left unanswered? Does the narrative ramble back and forth and lose impact? Is there a lot of repetition? Do you need a glossary? Footnotes? An appendix?
- In nonfiction, you may need to revise your outline, add explanations, decide how to define terms, remove excess or repetitive narrative, decide if you will use pull quotes, tables, graphs, or photos and if so, where those will be best placed.

At this stage you may end up moving scenes around or deleting some completely, writing new scenes, deleting or adding/changing/combining characters and their arcs, or modifying your beginning or ending. You may need to elaborate on actions or fix plot holes, or build up some scenes and condense others. Your pacing may be too fast or too slow, or inappropriate for the action in the scene. Your stakes and conflict may need more tension.

If you contract for a full developmental edit, you can expect the editor to mark up your manuscript using *Track Changes*, use *Comments* on the side, and possibly do some kind of Summary Report detailing the strengths and weaknesses of the project, along with specific suggestions for improvements.

A developmental edit can be particularly valuable for inexperienced writers and first-time authors, for those switching from nonfiction to fiction or vice versa, or for writers moving from shorter works like short stories or magazine articles to a book-length project for the first time. The things you learn in this edit can make you a better writer for all your future projects.

Instead of a full developmental edit, you might contract for a MANUSCRIPT CRITIQUE or EDITORIAL ASSESSMENT. Here an editor might provide a Summary of your work overall, or line by line notes, or both—with feedback on the positive *and* negative aspects of your story. Some will provide concrete suggestions. Others will just point out areas that need further development.

This might be a one-time edit or you may go back to the editor multiple times after implementing their suggestions to get everything working well. That may lead into coaching.

This edit might be your most expensive. When you sign with a developmental editor, be sure you understand what you will get for your money, and that it will be what your project needs and what you want. Have a detailed contract and be sure you understand it completely. If you don't, ask the editor to elaborate and clarify. Don't work with an editor who won't provide an explicit and detailed contract.

You may be able to accomplish some of this type of editing yourself during early revisions, and with the help of specifically-directed beta readers or critique partners or critique groups (described previously in *Early Self-Editing*).

SENSITIVITY & SPECIALTY READERS

Timeline varies.

These readers are now being used—and paid—by authors to ensure authenticity in writing characters who are unlike the author themselves, or writing situations that, due to lack of experience or a diversity of some kind, the author could not know about first-hand. It can be anything that an author has not experienced but wants to be particularly authentic.

One of my books had the characters at a polo match (the hero was playing polo) and, while I am a lifelong horsewoman who has had one polo lesson and offer specialty reads in how horses are used in a book, I have never seen a polo match in person and don't know the intricacies of the sport, so I put out an online request for anyone with first-hand expertise in polo to read that scene and let me know if it was authentic. I had offers from Australia, England, and France and their suggestions were spot-on. For one of my scenes set in Derbyshire, England—a place I have not yet been—I asked for input from those who lived there or had traveled there extensively to be sure I described the character's impressions of the landscape correctly. A book about a fictional race car driver might need a specialty reader to confirm accuracy of details, attitudes, fears, training, etc.

Sensitivity reads are often focused on differences like race, culture, neurodiversity, gender variations, ageism, mental or physical health conditions and the like. For example, one novel I edited had a side character who was a parent raising a child with Down Syndrome so the author had hired a sensitivity reader with personal experience with Down Syndrome to read the book and give her suggestions about keeping it real.

For my two-page polo scene, I offered each reader a free book. Two declined, saying they would rather buy the book to support me as an author, and the other wanted a free ebook. However, if the sensitivity or specialty reader needs to read more than a few pages they should definitely be paid a standard rate.

You would most likely use these readers in the earlier stages.

LINE OR STYLISTIC EDITING

Timeline 4-12 weeks.

A line editor goes through your manuscript line by line.

This is the stylistic or craft phase. It evaluates the tone, style, and consistency of your writing, and the way you use language to communicate to your reader. At this stage your plot, characters, writing tense, and point(s) of view are solid, as is organization/presentation. Your characters have effective arcs that work well with the plot arcs.

A line editor examines the language and addresses word choice, subtext (the meaning hidden beneath what is written and how it is written), use of literary devices (free indirect discourse, symbolism, imagery, simile, analogy, irony, hyperbole, etc.), syntax (how the arrangement of the words in a sentence conveys meaning), and overall sentence structure. Appropriateness of vocabulary and style for the intended audience/genre/era or world are assessed.

Here are some questions that line editing might address.

- Is it clear, fluid, and a pleasure to read?
- Do sentences have a pleasing rhythm and pulse that enhances the reading experience?
- Are paragraphs well structured? Do they flow logically?
- Does your writing effectively communicate a sense of atmosphere, emotion, and the tone intended?
- Have the best words been chosen to convey precise meaning? Or are boring verbs propped up by adverbs?
- Is use of language appropriately inclusive?
- Do you need one or more sensitivity or specialty readers?
- Does too much description bog down the action in a scene?
- Are there generalizations or cliches?
- Is dialogue realistic, and styled to differentiate the uniqueness of the characters?
- Is use of dialogue tags appropriate or distracting—and are there too many or not enough?
- Are transitions needed to connect abrupt jumps between passages or scenes?

- Are non-fiction terms explained? Would a glossary be helpful?
- Is clarity lost in too many words, or in jargon that will annoy or confuse your reader?
- Would pull-quotes help highlight significant points?
- Would an end-of-chapter takeaway or summary be user-friendly?

This edit will also make suggestions about showing versus telling, passive and active voice usage, appropriate pacing within scenes, consistency of voice and point(s) of view. The editor will flag head-hopping (when the point of view character is suddenly changed within a scene so the reader isn't clear who is speaking/thinking).

At this juncture scenes may still be deleted or altered, but if there is too much structural change needed, it is advised you return to the developmental stage until those issues are better resolved.

If the writer has fairly good literary skills in the above areas, some editors will combine a light line edit with a copy edit.

As you can see, line editing is quite extensive. Some of these items might be addressed in a copy edit, but be aware that if you contract for only a copy edit, you will miss out on feedback on most or all of the above issues. Many new writers are not even aware of these issues and may not understand how they impact the quality of their story or nonfiction book. These craft skills are what raise your writing to the next level.

Line editing is valuable, especially for authors with less literary experience. Writers can learn much from a good line edit that will improve not only their current book but also apply to all future writing. Think of line editing as an investment in yourself as a writer, as well as in your current and future projects.

COPYEDITING

Timeline 3-8 weeks.

This is the technical or mechanical phase of editing. Copyediting is what most people think of when they hear the word "editing." The copyeditor looks at all the small mechanical details of the work while keeping in mind the overarching theme and style of the piece.

THERE IS NO POINT IN PAYING FOR THIS STAGE OF EDITING IF YOU ARE STILL DOING REVISIONS IN THE ABOVE TWO STAGES.

Many authors are confused about the differences between copyediting and proofreading. They are *not* the same. The two are done at different levels of intensity and occur at a different time in the process, although they look for some of the same things.

Here are some of the issues addressed in a copyedit.

- Spelling, punctuation, referential pronoun usage, subject-verb agreement, use of proper tenses, consistency in spellings, numeral use, hyphenation (is it e-mail or email?), capitalizations (yes sir or yes Sir), and use of abbreviations. Some of these choices are stylistic, and the author will need to provide the editor with a brief—or create one with the editor's help so consistency can be maintained. When these items are incorrect, readers can be pulled out of the story by trying to figure out who is talking, or what happened to the yellow house, or if a scene is taking place in the present or in a flashback.

- Story and setting inconsistencies are pointed out. Is the house yellow in one chapter but gray in another? Does a character have blue eyes on page 5 and brown eyes on page 137? Was the person talking while walking outdoors then suddenly they are at the table eating? Do they suddenly speak to a person who wasn't in the scene?

- Are you mixing past tense and present tense incorrectly, causing reader confusion? Does the timeline in the scene make sense—is someone admiring a birthday cake that isn't made until a later scene? Is a fire burning brightly in the hearth when the characters enter, but a few paragraphs or pages later someone lights the fire?

- Do the Table of Contents titles agree with the chapter titles?

- Are footnotes correct, if used?

- Is there a glossary of terms? Is the method of identifying terms consistent?

- Are proper names spelled correctly and consistently?

Grammar software exists that can be helpful here, and its use might reduce your copyediting cost a bit, but software does not and cannot replace the human eye or brain. There are just too many nuances. (See *Let Basic Technology Work for You* later in this book.)

Some copyeditors also do fact-checking, but some do not. This definitely comes into play in nonfiction, but can also be relevant in fiction. Do you say your characters live during the Civil War but you have the year wrong? Is a character in the middle ages using the word "okay"? Do you have the correct king or queen ruling the country in the correct year? Be sure you know what you are getting as far as fact-checking per your contract.

Same with evaluation of unintentional libel or defamation, and liability issues such as use of lyrics or quotes or poems or copyrighted characters. Some copyeditors deal with these things, others don't. Read your contract carefully. Note: don't use song lyrics unless you have written permission from the current copyright holder and (likely) have paid to use them. Citing a source is not enough.

PROOFREADING

Timeline 2-3 weeks.

This is the final stage of editing, the last look at your manuscript before publication. Proofreading happens *after* your digital design of the covers (they need to be proofread too) and the interior is complete and formatting is done—if you are self-publishing. In addition to picking up odd typos that were missed in the copyediting phase, proofreading also checks that the layout, page numbering, and similar structural items are correct, and that no glitches have occurred in the formatting process. The proofreader looks for orphans and widows on the printed pages. Fonts, type sizes, paragraph spacing, indents, consistent and correct use of heads and subheads are all reviewed. Correct matching and positioning of artwork or photos and their captions are checked.

If you are an indie, you should of course proofread your final author's proof copy in printed form, but do also hire someone for a final proofread. We miss so many things in our own work, especially after we have read it literally dozens of times.

FORMATTING

Timeline varies.

Formatting is needed in order to digitally upload your book to the sales sites. For more information about formatting for the indie author, see the companion volume to my book—*About Writing and Self-Publishing, an essential guide for new authors* by Allie Cresswell.

There are various free and purchased ways to format (digitize). Most formatting programs or procedures work best on a Word document. You can learn to format yourself in Word, or you can use proprietary programs such as those at Reedsy or Amazon or Draft2Digital. You can buy formatting software, such as Vellum (my choice). Or you can hire a professional formatter.

Formatting is important because this is where the design of your pages happens. Page design has a lot to do with legibility and a reader's enjoyment of your book, their recommendation of your book, and their loyalty to you and your books.

Layouts for novels are fairly standard, but nonfiction books, poetry collections, or other more creative works may require special expertise for charts, pull quotes, and other layout devices.

Some editors do formatting (I do), and many will have connections with formatters so they are able to direct you to someone reputable.

PROCESSING YOUR EDITS

Please don't be discouraged by the number of editing marks on your digital manuscript when it is returned to you. First-time writers are especially sensitive about this, and understandably. But don't panic. You are paying for a service and you want it to be thorough. Just take a deep breath and trust it will all work out well in the end. If you've chosen a good editor, it will.

Many authors read over the markup and then take a week or more to "digest" the changes, at which time their panic reaction has subsided. It doesn't mean you're not a good writer. It likely means you have a good editor. And if you do, some of those comments are likely compliments!

Authors have different work flows for processing their edits and you will likely work out what is best for you. But here are some guidelines to keep in mind.

- Some authors like to keep an unaltered copy of the manuscript with all the edits intact, as received from the editor. Then they make a different copy of the markup that will be their new working copy in which they will accept or reject the edits and make changes per the comments on the side.

- Some authors use two screens to make changes on their original master copy while looking at the editor's marked up version.
- Whatever system you choose, be sure to *label your different documents clearly!* You don't want to think you're in your newest working copy when you're accidentally in the editor's copy, or in your own original submission-to-editor copy! This is crucial because processing the edits will take several work sessions and you don't want to forget which version you were working on.
- Take care to back up (in multiples) everything you have touched at the end of each work session. If you lose some corrections, it can be very confusing to try to work out what is what and where to pick up.

Go slowly, label accurately, and back up.

SUMMARY

Your book may not need all these levels of editing—it depends on your skills and your strengths as a writer. That decision may also depend on your budget. The decision also depends on your goals for this particular book, and your goals for your writing career.

With the right kind of editing at the right time, your book will have a better chance of success, whether your intention is to inform, to entertain, or to commemorate.

chapter
six

Finding & Choosing an Editor

YOUR EDITOR IS a member of your publishing team. You will be working together closely. Choose someone you can get along with and who you believe is trustworthy.

Expect that a good editor will be booked 1-6 months in advance.

Plan ahead.

Where does one find an editor? Here are some suggestions.

- *Word-of-mouth recommendations* can be the best source for finding an editor. Ask *successful* writers or members of your writing group or of any genre association of which you are a member who they recommend for editing. Look at that person's book to get an idea of the quality of the editing that was done.
- *Social media sites* can be sources of editor names to put on your list to investigate. Be active on these writer sites. Editing is often talked about and people post

questions and recommendations, and some sites allow editors to post their website in the comments. Some sites have a list of editors posted. Be aware these are likely not vetted, just listed.

- Some professional associations have lists of vetted editors, such as The Alliance of Independent Authors, Reedsy, Editorial Freelance Association, ACES, and more. Writers can access these lists for free.

- Work sites like Fiverr and Upwork also list editors. While there may be some good editors on these sites, be sure to vet them very carefully. Most good editors are booked ahead and don't need to list themselves (and pay part of their fee) to sites like this. And remember, if the price sounds too good to be true, it's probably something to pass up.

- Look for editing credits in successful books in your genre. Editor credits are usually found on the copyright page or in the acknowledgements section. But do be aware that the author has the final word on which edits to accept and use, so the final book may be altered significantly from what the editor recommended.

Hiring an editor can be an intimidating step. Up until now, it's just been you, researching and writing and revising. Maybe you involved beta readers, who are usually unpaid. But now you will be adding a professional team member, a legal contract—and money will be involved. It begins to get very real very fast, especially with your first book.

Proceed with awareness after having done your due diligence in learning about editing and carefully choosing your editor candidates. You are hiring someone for their expert opinion and professional knowledge—rather like choosing a personal medical care provider. But remember, it is still your book and you are still in charge (until or if you sign with an agent and/or publisher). You don't have to accept all the edits. Don't be blindly stubborn about accepting critique, but don't be blind to your own knowledge about your book either. As a wonderful pediatrician once told me, "You know your child better than I do. You are the expert. I am simply here to share my advanced knowledge and show you some options." (Thank you, Dr. Viehweg.)

Many first-time authors worry about an editor stealing their work. I believe this is extremely rare. A good editor wants to stay in business, and get repeat business. They want to maintain a good reputation. To alleviate this fear, do your due diligence and vet your editor candidates thoroughly.

Your work is copyrighted the moment you write it. When your work is in final form you can register this copyright with the government for a fee. That simply makes things a little easier should you ever have to go to court or haggle with a sales site about being the true author. With writing now done on computer and the date/time stamps on all your versions of your book, proving that you are the author is easier than it used to be. Note that I said wait until your book is in its *final* form and published to register your copyright.

When you approach an editor, or inquire in an online group for recommendations, it helps if you state your genre, your word count, the type of editing you think you need, and any pertinent scheduling information. Your responses will then be more appropriately narrow. For example, if your book is horror and I don't edit horror (or my editor doesn't), I won't respond to that group post. If you want only proofreading and I specialize in line editing, I won't respond. If you want editing done within the next 60 days and I am booked for four months, I won't respond. It streamlines communication for everyone.

Here are some important considerations as you research and choose an editor.

- *Be sure you are in agreement regarding communication style* before you go further. Many editors insist on communication via email. This protects both of you. With an electronic trail, either of you can refer back to what was "discussed." Some editors offer a virtual meeting before or after completion of the project. Some will work with you by phone. Others won't.
- *Visit the editor's website and/or Facebook page.* Does it look modern and professional or perhaps it's appropriate to a genre they might specialize in, such as fantasy or historical or children's books? Is the website well organized? Are there typos? Their website is likely a representation of the quality of work they do. And if

they have no social media presence—that could be a red flag.

- *Decide if you want someone who charges by the word or by the project.* Either is acceptable and both have their pros and cons. Do not choose someone who charges by the page. They are not a professional and likely don't know what they're doing. By hiring someone who charges per word, you will pay the same for your fairly clean manuscript as someone else would for a manuscript that's a hot mess. Personally, I don't feel this is fair to authors and I don't charge this way. I charge by the project, which takes into account the condition of your manuscript—so if you have done your prep well and completed some of your own editing and revised wisely, you will likely save money with a "project" estimate instead of a per-word charge. But per-word has long been a standard too.

- *Know what kind of editing you want or think you need.* This depends on what stage you are at in the writing process. If you don't know what your project needs, ask the editor to give you a recommendation when they do a sample edit. The different types of editing come at different price points. Proofreading is usually the least expensive, and developmental or line editing are usually the most expensive.

- *Be sure your editor does the type of editing you want.* Some do only copyediting, some do only developmental editing, etc. You may need to hire a different editor for each type of editing you want done. There are pros and cons to having the same editor for your whole project, one who gets to know your work well, or having a fresh set of eyes for each different edit. Some like to hire a different editor for a final proofread—one who hasn't seen your work before. That can be effective. But that's not absolutely necessary. It is helpful to establish a strong writer/editor relationship with someone you trust. I give a discount to my repeat customers because the whole flow is more efficient when we know how each other works.

- *Get a sample edit* from at least three editors on the same 1000 words. Some do this for free (I do), and some charge for this, but it is really helpful in determining what your project needs if you're not sure. It's also a good way to see if you and the editor mesh well, and if they understand your book and your vision for it. Compare the differences in what each editor points out, their thoroughness, their timeliness, their price, their pleasantness to work with, and the balance between how many edits you don't agree with to how many you find useful. You don't want to pay for a lot of edits you will discard.

- *Choose someone who has recent experience in your genre.* An academic/scientific editor would not be the best choice to edit a romance novel. Nor would an editor who specializes in romance novels be the best person to edit historical nonfiction. One editor might do general fiction but no nonfiction. Another might specialize in YA (young adult). Another might prefer to work on thrillers. Some have types of work they prefer not to edit, such as horror. Others specialize in horror. Books for children require special knowledge to edit.

- *A professional editor will use Microsoft Word's Track Changes feature* for your edit. If they don't use this, they are likely not very knowledgeable or up to date with modern literary style and practices. The exception might be in developmental editing where an editor may offer a report instead, or a summary of some kind. Some editors will work with Google Docs or other formats, but Word is the gold standard at present.
- *Choose an editor who offers a contract.* This protects both of you. All terms, conditions, possible default scenarios, types of editing, costs, deadlines, etc. should be clear in the contract. If they won't offer you a comprehensive signed and dated contract, they are not professional, and may be a scammer. Walk away. There are plenty of qualified editors to be found, at a variety of price points.
- *Be aware of standard practices and procedures* in the editing world so you can make the best decision for your book. *(See next chapter for details.)*

If editing boggles your mind and you really can't recognize quality editing yourself, go over your sample edits with someone who reads a great deal or has some knowledge of grammar, such as an English teacher. But do be aware that an English teacher is not an editor. Members of your writing group can also be helpful with evaluating your free sample edits.

In the end, you are the author and it is your project. Your editor is to your manuscript as your doctor is to your body. Both offer professional expertise but you make the final choices.

Choose wisely.

chapter
seven

Standard Practices & Procedures

IT SHOULD GO without saying that having a professional edit done does not guarantee your work will be published by a traditional publisher, or that it will be a top seller in the self-publishing world. But professional editing greatly increases your chance of recognition and success.

The following are standard practices in the professional editing industry.

- You will most likely be required to *pay a deposit* to hold your slot once you have chosen an editor. This will be credited against your first up-front payment, although some part of it may be nonrefundable because if you cancel at the last moment, the editor may not be able to fill that slot with another job. What does your contract say?
- *Expect to pay 1/3 to 1/2 up front* to your editor when you return your signed contract. This is industry

standard. When your edit is finished, the editor will invoice you for the balance due. After you pay this balance, you will receive your edited manuscript. Again, this is industry standard. This is also why you should choose a known professional you can trust, and have a sample edit done so you know what to expect.

- Understand that *you will likely not see your project until it is completed*. Some editors will make exceptions for long projects or with repeat clients. Your editor is working on a comprehensive project and generally needs to work with it *as a whole*, not piece by piece. Your initial brief to the editor and your contract should lay out your expectations and what you have agreed to do.

- *Edits might need to be reviewed or discussed later.* The specifics of this should also be included in your contract. Many editors allow 30-60 minutes to discuss the completed project. Many include their reasoning or explanations of edits in the *Comments* section on the side margin in Word. Talk about this before you sign your contract so you are both clear. It is always the author's prerogative to accept changes/suggestions or not.

- *How will you pay?* Does the editor accept checks? Credit cards? Various online payment services like PayPal or Venmo? Some editors offer payment plans. Some will allow monthly payments. Again, get all payment arrangements in writing, signed and dated in your contract.

- Your contract should include *what happens if either party defaults* on the contract. In detail. People get sick or become unable to work. Cover all possible scenarios.
- The contract should also have a *confidentiality clause.* No editor should use your work on their website or in a training without your explicit written permission.
- This also applies in reverse. *Please don't credit your editor on your copyright page or acknowledgements page without their written permission.* Their professional reputation is at stake. Once the editor returns your manuscript to you, they have no way of knowing which edits you kept and which you discarded. They don't know if you've deleted or added sections or rewritten half the book, or had someone else edit it afterward. If you are so pleased with your editor's work that you want to give them a shout-out, just ask first. You can also offer to write a *testimonial* they could use with their marketing materials or on their website. And you can recommend them on social media sites.

Knowing and complying with standard professional practices makes the whole editing process easier and less apt to result in unexpected or unwelcome situations. You are paying good money for this service, so keep it professional author to professional editor.

chapter
eight

Your Path to Publishing Determines Your Editing Needs

BEFORE YOU HIRE AN EDITOR, it is helpful to know which publishing path you plan to pursue—or at least to have an idea. I will address these choices from an editing perspective.

———

DO BE AWARE THAT IF YOU CHOOSE INDIE PUBLISHING, THE GATE IS THEN CLOSED TO TRADITIONAL PUBLISHING FOR THAT PARTICULAR BOOK UNLESS YOU HAPPEN TO SELL TENS OF THOUSANDS OF THAT BOOK.

———

TRADITIONAL PUBLISHING

This is the old familiar standard, where an agent agrees to represent you to a publisher, who then offers you a contract and maybe a monetary advance to publish your book. Most of the bigger publishers now require that you have an agent; they no longer deal directly with authors.

The traditional publisher handles all the publishing tasks—*at their own expense*—such as editing, formatting (interior page design and digitizing), cover design, and sometimes some marketing guidance, although nowadays every author should plan to do their own marketing. Besides the "Big Five" publishers (which are always changing as they buy each other out, consolidate, and add divisions), there are some small traditional publishers that are legitimate who also provide *all* the publishing tasks at no charge to the author.

IN TRADITIONAL PUBLISHING, THE AUTHOR PAYS NOTHING UP FRONT. This is very important to remember. *The author pays nothing.*

In exchange for fronting all the publishing costs, the publisher essentially leases the rights to use your book for a set number of years in a set number of ways (print, digital, film, audio, etc.) and pays you, the author, a percentage of sales (gross or net or whatever formula that publisher follows). This is usually around 5% to 12% for print books, and varies for ebooks but is often 25% as of this writing. Agents in the US get paid 15% of the author's royalties so *their cut comes out of your 5-12%.*

For the author, traditional publishing means:

- less financial outlay up front (some editing is needed to clear the acceptance hurdle)
- possibly larger audience reach and distribution
- good production quality, usually
- a long timeline for the publishing process (1-3 years)

- a big hurdle to get the publisher and/or agent to choose you from among thousands of others hoping to be traditionally published
- deadlines imposed that you must meet, such as rewrites or edit approvals
- less control over your book's contents and covers
- a smaller piece of a potentially but not guaranteed larger pie

Editing tasks still exist on the traditional path and are important. They are usually limited to your submission materials in order to get accepted/signed. After that, editing at your own expense would be limited to any marketing materials you create—and your website. Read your publishing contract to confirm these arrangements.

- Your manuscript needs to be written well enough—with few to no grammatical errors—to impress an agent or publisher so they will take you on. Remember, the competition is fierce.
- For fiction, your query letter, synopsis, and sample chapters are part of the QUERY PACKAGE you send to agents or publishers as you seek representation. These all need to be error-free and of high quality.
- Nonfiction books do not need to be completed to submit a proposal. For nonfiction, you create a BOOK PROPOSAL PACKAGE that consists of whatever the agent or publisher wishes to see (outline, table of contents, marketing plan, sample chapters,

author expertise on the topic and the author platform and number of followers are commonly wanted). All these submission items should be error-free and well-written. Again, competition is fierce.

You will have to invest time to research and figure out which agents or publishers among hundreds are the best fit for you, learn what they want to see, and then create and submit your query or proposal package to them individually. You can't send the same letter or information to them all, it must be tailored to each specifically. Depending on how niche your book is, you may be sending to over one hundred prospects.

If you get a publishing contract (which can take a couple of years to secure), your publisher's editors will work on your project with you so it meets the specs of that publishing house. They will edit the book to make it what they determine is most marketable. The amount of input you have during this process varies, but the publisher is paying for everything so they have the final say.

TRADITIONAL PUBLISHING MAKES ITS MONEY FROM BOOK SALES—*NOT* FROM THE AUTHOR. *None of it from the author.*

INDIE PUBLISHING

Imagine yourself as a general contractor and your book as a new house to be built. As an indie you have the responsibility for the overall project. You write it, design it, direct it, market it. You hire subcontractors such as editors and cover designers and formatters. You pay them the going rates. *(Note that these are all tax deductions—even before you publish—if you have set yourself up as a business. Please consult a tax preparer or an accountant.)*

You have the final word on which edits you accept or reject, and you make the final choices on cover design and interior design. You create the marketing strategy and implement it. And all the income is yours!

As an indie author, you will have a monetary outlay up front, usually for editing and for cover design at least. There are ways to minimize these expenses, as I have explained.

You will earn a much higher royalty as an indie author. Sales sites take their cut of your book sales for listing your book in various places. They take their cut off the sales. There is no up-front cost to the author to put your book up to sell once it is properly prepared. You end up making about 70% of the retail price for ebooks, and anywhere from 30% to 70% on your print books. And *you* set your own prices and wholesale discounts.

IT'S IMPORTANT TO NOTE THAT NO MATTER WHICH PUBLISHING PATH YOU TAKE, PROMOTION AND MARKETING WILL BE LARGELY UP TO YOU. THE DAYS OF A NEW AUTHOR GETTING A BIG ADVANCE AND BEING SENT ON A GLAMOROUS BOOK TOUR AT THE PUBLISHER'S EXPENSE ARE NO MORE.

Of course, you have expenses to account for. But a good product will keep selling long after you have broken even on your costs. It then becomes passive income.

You will also pay printing costs (and shipping) for paperback or hardcover books that you might sell at events or from your website. These costs are tax deductible, usually as cost of goods sold, but please consult your tax preparer or accountant, as I am neither and cannot offer you specific advice.

There are multiple retail and wholesale stores from which to sell your book worldwide. Amazon (KDP), Ingram Spark, Apple, Kobo, Barnes & Noble, Google, and Draft 2 Digital are some of them. Some of these are retail (sell direct to the customer), some are wholesalers (sell to bookstores who resell), and some are aggregators (sell ebooks to other retail sites at a smaller-than-wholesale cut.) There is no charge to list your book on these sites. If you never sell a book, you pay nothing to upload or be on their site.

For the author, indie publishing means:

- more financial outlay to pay subcontractors such as editors
- more time and effort on your part to hire and coordinate your subcontractors
- higher financial returns per sale
- more financial tracking and business management tasks
- business expense tax deductions that can offset income from your day job *(consult a tax preparer or accountant for details)*

- a much faster timeline until publication—and you set the timeline
- you set deadlines, but they will need to coordinate with what you set for your hired subcontractors
- complete control of your content, your project, and your career

On the indie path, editing is crucial. If your book is full of errors (or your website or marketing materials are), your name and brand are tarnished forever and your sales will reflect this.

As an indie, you will need an editor for your manuscript (maybe more than one editor), as well as editing for your book page on the sales platforms, for your website, and for your marketing materials and book covers. I am amazed at how many book covers I see with obvious typos!

INDIE PUBLISHING MAKES MONEY DIRECTLY FROM BOOK SALES, *AND* FROM ANY PERIPHERAL SALES YOU CREATE *(tee shirts? dolls? templates?)*, *AND* FROM RELATED THINGS YOU MIGHT CHOOSE TO DO *(consult or speak about your topic? lead workshops?)* You won't need permission from anyone to experiment with various marketing strategies. You are the boss. You pay all the expenses, you reap all the rewards.

⊏⊐

For more in-depth self-publishing guidance, get the companion book to this one—Allie Cresswell's *About Self-Publishing, an essential guide for new authors*. She has self-published fourteen books and goes into detail about how to do it all and what's worked for her.

HYBRID PUBLISHERS, SERVICE PROVIDERS, AND VANITY PRESSES

This is a murky path so tread here with caution. None of these are publishers or presses in the real sense because *you are paying them*. It's murky because it is very difficult to distinguish between a real hybrid press, a quality service provider, and the scam companies flooding the marketplace and your inbox. If they aggressively hound you, they are likely not legitimate. Proceed with care.

Although contracts vary, HYBRID PRESSES seem to require you to pay a percentage of the total production costs up front (but sometimes you don't know what that total is!), then they share the royalties with you. They may or may not hold your copyright. Sometimes you are required to buy a certain number of books from them, at prices much higher than the cost of author copies direct from the other sales sites like KDP or Ingram. They may own the covers and the formatted interiors they have created, unless your contract says otherwise. You may pay exorbitant fees for interior changes or corrections, or to add new books to your "back matter" section, and for them to upload the changes—all of which you can do yourself for free as an indie. Again, read your contract carefully and know what's included and what isn't.

A true hybrid press does not accept all authors. Like a traditional press, they are very choosy about who they work with because they, too, are investing money and time.

A HYBRID PRESS MAKES MONEY IN TWO WAYS—

FROM SALES OF YOUR BOOK *AND* FROM WHAT YOU PAY THEM UP FRONT. THE MORE BOOKS SOLD, THE MORE MONEY YOU BOTH MAKE. At least that's the idea.

The next two paths of publishing tend to appeal to an author's ego with their marketing strategy. They praise your writing, yet will publish anything, no matter how poorly written.

AUTHOR SERVICE PROVIDERS usually offer a "package" of services to authors, including editing, cover design, formatting, and uploading to a sales site, but usually at a rate far higher than independent service providers charge. The quality may be poor— the editing I have seen from these service providers is appalling. The appeal is the convenience of services all in one package, but do know there are freelancers who can provide the same things for much less money. Service providers usually don't take any royalties, and they leave your copyright completely with you. They may "own" the cover design and the formatted interior—maybe even the edited interior they created—so if you want to go elsewhere or indie, you'll have to pay for these services all over again. Check your contract. You are usually charged high fees to make interior changes or corrections, or to add new books to your "back matter" section, and then charged to upload the changes—all things you can do yourself for free as an indie. These ongoing expenses can bleed you. Read your contract carefully.

SERVICE PROVIDERS MAKE THEIR MONEY *COMPLETELY FROM AUTHORS.* THEY HAVE NO

VESTED INTEREST IN PRODUCING A SELLABLE BOOK. This alone should give you pause.

VANITY PRESSES (so named because they appeal to the vanity of the author who desperately wants to be published) are the worst possible choice from an editing perspective—and from any perspective. They provide the typical services for a very high fee but usually of low quality. They hold your publishing rights— sometimes for a certain number of years, but sometimes when you sign with them you are signing over your rights to your book, forever. It can be very difficult or impossible to get those rights back. Besides having you pay *all* the publication expenses, they also take a share of the royalties. Many authors never receive any royalties at all. A vanity press may masquerade as a service provider or a hybrid press. Vanity presses will hound you once they get your contact information.

Any author can do better than using a vanity press. Ask in online writing groups if you have questions about a company.

VANITY PRESSES MAKE THEIR MONEY FROM AUTHORS *AND* FROM BOOK SALES, if there are any sales reported.

chapter
nine
Learn the Craft

MOST AUTHORS genuinely want to learn the craft of writing and improve their skills. There are lots of online opportunities to learn. Besides grammar knowledge, authors need writing knowledge to write well and effectively. The better your skills, the less editing your work will need.

Some webinars are free, although at the end they may try to sell you their book or their course. Still, you can learn a lot without purchasing those.

Some webinars are low-cost ($25 seems reasonable to me) and you sometimes get lifetime access to the content. I have found Jane Friedman's sessions can always be relied upon, and there are many others available too. Places like Reedsy and some sales sites like Draft2Digital and Ingram Spark have author webinars. Be alert for these opportunities to learn. *And remember, these costs are tax deductions.*

You can also join genre associations. I am a member of the Women's Fiction Writers Association. These groups often put on webinars or conferences addressing specific skills or knowledge needed.

Be picky about what you spend time or money learning, and don't plunk down big chunks of money for a "success overnight" scam. There are hundreds of those!

Get active in online writing groups—you can learn a lot there too. Just be sure you vet the information shared as it won't all be reliable.

———

Here are some "craft" topics and skills to consider as you review your work. These will help you learn skills and better evaluate your own writing. The more of these issues you can deal with yourself, the more money you will save on editing.

- *Every scene of the story should move the plot ahead* or deepen the reader's knowledge or understanding of a character. If it does not, change it or add to it or delete it.
- *Learn the basics of point of view (POV).* You probably write in first person or third person (which can be deep or more omniscient). Second person is rarely used, but has its place. Stay in the head of your POV character. If you write multiple POV characters, be sure you transition appropriately and don't just "head hop" into another character's thoughts in the middle of a scene. That confuses the reader.

- *Develop your knowledge of tenses and their variations.* Tenses can be confusing. Many writers seem to confuse tense with point of view. Tenses are about time. They are different from point of view, which is about who is speaking and how. You can write in first person—in present tense or in past tense. You can write in third person—in present tense or past tense. In present tense the action is happening now, as the reader reads it ("I see him"). This is especially popular for certain genres, such as middle grade and YA. You may write in past tense ("I saw him"). Then there are the nuances of tense needed in certain situations, such as slipping into a memory sequence using past perfect to enter and to exit the passage ("I had seen him.") When I edit, I see a lot of problems with tenses. The wrong ones muddle your story; the right ones lend clarity.

- *Be sure your nouns and verbs agree regarding singular and plural.* Certain inserted phrases can make this confusing. You need to sort out which noun is actually the subject. If the noun is plural, the verb needs to be plural.

- *Know how and where to use the correct referential pronoun.* This is one of the most common errors I see. Here's an example. "Susan left for the concert, intending to meet Judy there. When she arrived, her friend was nowhere to be found." Who is "she" in this sentence? Grammatically, a pronoun refers back to the last-named person, which is Judy. But logic tells us that it was Susan who arrived and couldn't find her friend. This kind of error can really throw your readers off and pull them out of the story as they try to figure out who is being referred to. As the writer, it's clear in your head, but not necessarily for the reader.

- *Understand the difference between showing and telling.* Don't tell your reader the moon lit up the room. Show how it reflects on a glass vase or a mirror. Don't tell the reader your character is angry. Describe his scowl, show him balling up his fists until his nails leave marks.

- In nonfiction your *narration should be clear and consistent, with a "voice" that will appeal to your audience.*

- *Make sure your structure and organization are strong and concise.*

- *Learn how to write realistic, meaningful dialogue.* Give each character a distinct voice. Is your dialogue natural or stilted? Don't "info-dump" within dialogue, it's unnatural.

- *Use dialogue tags only when needed* to determine who is speaking (if the action beats don't clarify this). Use "said" or "asked" for most dialog tags—they become "invisible" in the narrative and don't draw attention to themselves. You want the attention to be on the dialogue itself, not the tag. Don't get creative with dialog tags. Instead, make the dialogue itself creative.

- *Use action beats to demonstrate who is talking and what they mean.* Paint a picture of how the character looks and acts. Have him pound his fist on the table or stomp out of the room when he speaks. For example, "His eyes spit fire. 'You'll regret this,' he said, then turned on his heel and was gone." You don't have to say he is angry, you've showed it. Be sure you are showing these actions, not just telling about the actions.

- *If you are in deep POV you don't need "he thought" or "she noticed."* These words clog up the flow of the narrative. And internal dialogue usually doesn't need to be in italics; that is considered dated now in most cases.

- *Listen to the rhythm of your writing.* Are the sentences of varying lengths? Do they become short and clipped when action is high? Do they become languorous or relaxed to slow down the pace? A good rhythm makes for more interesting reading and better comprehension.

- *Don't rely on filter words.* They increase narrative distance and hold the reader away from actually experiencing the story. "He began to walk" vs "He walked." "She seemed to feel her heart beginning to beat hard" vs "Her heart beat hard." Examples of filter words: noticed, seems, saw, spotted, feels, realized, wondered, thought, believed, knew, decided. Most 'ing' words also distance the reader. "She began running down the hill" vs "She ran down the hill." (And "ran" is a weak verb, you can do better—try raced or bolted or stumbled.)

- *Don't info-dump anywhere.* As the author, you know the detailed background of your setting and characters. You may have written a lot of it down. All of this knowledge is not needed by the reader, especially not all at once. Weave it into your narrative when needed for the reader to fully understand what is happening. Otherwise leave it out.
- *Don't solve the puzzle for the reader.* Don't tell them what to suspect or what to think. Don't point out clues, just give them. Readers like to discover the clues and make their own predictions and conclusions— that is the fun of reading.
- *Does your book start in the right place?* Often when we write, the first paragraphs are a way to ease into the story, which may actually start 500 or 2500 words into the manuscript. Don't spend too many words on background, description, or world building—include just enough to orient the reader. Weave in more as the reader needs to know more.
- *Is your point of view clear and strong?* Is it the best POV for your story? If using multiple POVs, is there a transition and is it clear to the reader?
- *Does the theme of your fiction or the point of your nonfiction come through clearly?*
- *Does every scene or section pull the reader through to the next one?*
- *Repetition weakens the narrative,* unless it is a deliberate echo.

- *Don't use multiple descriptors*—each additional descriptor dilutes the others. Choose one or two concise words.
- *Use strong specific verbs.* "Went" and "walked" can be much improved upon. Don't rely on adverbs—especially -ly words—to support weak generic verbs.

If your head is spinning after all this—congratulations! You have entered the mind of an editor. It really is a quite intense job, but very rewarding.

chapter
ten

Is Your Manuscript Ready for a Professional Editor?

A CHECKLIST

Go through this list to be sure you have done all you can before sending your manuscript to a professional editor. There really is a lot you can do yourself.

- Is your manuscript in the proper format? (12-point Times Roman, double spaced, one-inch margins, single space after periods)
- Did you set up your manuscript using *Style Sheets* in Word, including any indents and line spacing?
- Have you had and incorporated input from at least two beta readers?
- Have you read your manuscript aloud or had it read aloud to you?
- Have you made at least three revising/editing passes on your manuscript? (Ten is not uncommon!)
- Do you know what kind of editing you want or need?

- Have you searched for and removed extra returns, extra spaces after a period, and extra periods?
- Have you used Word's capabilities to check your manuscript for consistency in spellings (especially names)?
- Have you checked for *crutch words, filter words,* and excess use of *that*?
- Have you used the Craft list (*previous chapter*) and done your best to work through those issues? The more of these tasks you can do yourself, the more money you will save on your edit (unless you are paying by the word).

chapter
eleven

Are You Ready to Sign with an
Editor?

ANOTHER CHECKLIST

Be sure you have done your due diligence in vetting your editor candidates. Choose three or four. If none of those pan out, try to figure out why you chose them, and use different criteria for choosing your next three or four.

- Do your candidates perform the type of editing you think you want?
- Did you get three sample edits from editors who have experience in your genre and whose schedule and budget work with yours?
- Did you check out the editor's references and/or testimonials?
- Does the editor work with a contract? Will they let you see a sample of their contract?
- Do their financial terms suit your budget?

- Do they offer some type of review or support for your questions on edits?
- Do they seem like someone you would like to work closely with?

chapter
twelve

Be an Agreeable Client

THIS WILL GO a long way in building a mutually-beneficial relationship with your editor.

- Be pleasant. Be respectful. Be professional.
- Be open-minded and ready to learn.
- *Acknowledge receipt of your sample edit*, even if you are choosing a different editor. We really don't like to spend time and effort on a free sample edit, send it off, and never hear anything back! *Don't ghost us, please!* Here are two examples of what to say if you are undecided or are going with a different editor. "Thank you for the sample edit. I found it very helpful. Can we visit more about terms?" OR "Thank you for the sample edit. After careful consideration I have chosen to work with a different editor."

- Only ask for a sample edit when you are really ready for editing. Most editors offer just one free sample edit per project.
- Follow the terms and communication style you agreed to.
- Submit your project on time—*all of it*—unless other arrangements are made ahead of time and written into your contract.
- Be available while your project is being edited. Keep your cell phone with you for calls or texts. Check your email at least two or three times per day. If a question or problem arises that the editor needs to discuss with you but can't reach you, that can set the entire schedule back.
- Pay on time and as agreed.

chapter
thirteen

In Summary

I HOPE you found this book helpful but not overwhelming. There are so many misconceptions floating around about editing that I felt a basic book would answer a lot of questions.

This is a book for authors, not editors. There are many good, comprehensive books for editors about editing, but not many that explain, in common working terms, the ins and outs of editing for authors.

You don't need to know everything about editing to be a good author.

You do need to understand how important editing is to any written project, and how to choose the correct type of editing at the right time.

And how to find the right editor.

Once you find an editor you like working with, cultivate that relationship. It will benefit all your future writing projects and your author career.

thank you for reading this book!

I hope you, as an author, found it a useful tool to better understand the role of professional editing in your book's success, and the importance of a good author/editor relationship to your writing career.

As an author, you know the importance of book reviews. I would be grateful if you could take a few moments to write a quick online review—it helps me know if I reached my goal in helping authors. And your review might help another author decide if this book would benefit them.

For more information about my editing services and to read testimonials go to

www.quinnediting.com

acknowledgements

Every book creation involves a team and I would like to thank my team members:

- My friend Allie Cresswell, author of the companion book to this book, *About Self-Publishing, an essential guide for new authors*. Allie and I met in an online Facebook group while posting comments about Jane Austen's novels. I have now edited several of Allie's books, and when she told me about this newest project and asked about my editing expertise for it, I pulled this volume off my back burner and finished it. With her living in England and me in the US, we have never met in person. Hopefully that meeting is in our future.
- My beta readers and proofreaders: Allie Cresswell, Hazel Dahl Behrens, E. Goetz, Mikiya Goetz, Heidi Herman, and FJ.
- My talented cover designer: Rachael Ritchey.

about the author

Sallianne Hines writes contemporary and historical women's fiction, along with nonfiction works addressing issues of simple intentional living. Her books are available in ebook, paperback, and large print paperback formats.

Sallianne established Quinn Editing in 2015. She is a lifelong horsewoman, mother of three and grandmother of eight. When not writing or editing you might find her walking her dogs, in conversation with her cat, reading, knitting, sewing, gardening, sketching, tending her plants, and watching the wild birds she feeds—anything to avoid washing the dishes.

For more information, visit
www.salliannehines.com
www.quinnediting.com

other books written by sallianne hines

CURRENTLY AVAILABLE:

Love & Stones

Her Summer at Pemberley—Kitty Bennet's story

About Editing, an essential guide for authors

UPCOMING BOOKS:

The Pleasure of Her Company—Mrs. Dashwood's story

Her Time to Fly—Margaret Dashwood's story

Simply Dressed

Simply Grown

For more information about my books and me as an author, I invite you to visit my website

www.salliannehines.com

Made in the USA
Monee, IL
01 September 2023

41974101R00049